A TASTE OF INDONESIA

Edited by

Kenneth Mitchell

This edition published for

Oracle Book Distributors
257 Gloucester Road, Hong Kong.

ISBN 962 224 011 9

Printed in Hong Kong

Introduction

Indonesia is the world's largest archipelago, consisting of almost fourteen thousand islands, stretching over five thousand kilometres and forming a virtual 'land bridge' between Asia and Australia. Archaeologists have established man's existence in these islands to be more than half a million years and since those days of 'Java man' many races have arrived here; some to settle; some to colonise; some to trade; and some to plunder but, all to leave their mark. Malays, Mongols, Chinese, Arabs, Indians and Europeans; Buddhists, Hindus, Muslims and Christians; all have been here with their varied creeds, customs and cultures and all have brought, among other things, their culinary 'secrets' to add to the local produce and spices and, so create taste sensations second to none.

There is neither the space, nor the intent, in this small book to trace the culinary heritage of Indonesia. This edition is meant only to present a selection of 'end results' and so, hopefully, whet your appetite for a food style less well known than other Asian cuisines. The recipes were nearly all collected from professional chefs and, in some cases, I've made small changes to allow for eaiser preparation in foreign domestic kitchens. These days most ingredients are available worldwide and, where they are not, an inventive cook will always find an acceptable substitute (after all, that's how new flavours are discovered).

The national religion is Muslim and so, throughout most of the country, outside of Chinese restaurants and international hotels, pork is seldom served. However, the island of Bali is predominately Hindu, where the 'taboo' is beef and, the aroma of succulent barbecued pork is an added gastronomic attraction. Apart from the meats, the local waters abound with a wide variety of seafood and these, together with poultry and an incredible selection of vegetables and fruits, offer delights for every palate. There are, though, two common denominators for all. Firstly, the wonderful spices, for which these islands are so famed, are used liberally by cooks from northernmost Sumatra to the most southerly tip of West Irian and, secondly (it almost goes without saying) there is rice . . .

As with other Asian countries, the staple food of Indonesia is rice and the plain steamed variety is served at almost every meal, regardless of what else is being eaten. A great favourite is 'Nasi Goreng', the local name for fried rice, but it's more than the name implies and is often served as a complete meal, accompanied by crispy fried chicken legs, assorted sates, prawn crackers, green salad and a side-dish of sambal. Occasionally, even, with a fried egg on top. During the time the Dutch were in the country they added the world Rijstafel to the local culinary language. The literal translation is 'rice table' and this has become the name given to the exotic buffets, consisting of a multitude of dishes and served on special occasions. The Rijstafel is very popular with Western visitors as it gives the chance to sample a wide variety of tastes at one sitting (weight watchers beware!).

If there is such a thing as a 'national' dish in these far-flung islands, then it must be 'Sate', delicious 'sticks' of meat (beef, mutton or pork) or chicken or prawns, all marinated in spices, cooked over hot charcoal and dipped in a tasty peanut sauce. Sate can be enjoyed everywhere throughout the country, at small roadside stalls or in five star hotels and at all times; for breakfast, lunch or as a late night snack. For the all-important sauce, there must be literally hundreds of recipes and every cook *knows* his to be the best. Perhaps, you will improve on the one I offer.

SELAMAT MAKAN

Ingredients:

Notes on six ingredients, which are often used in Indonesian cooking, and which may be unfamiliar to some readers, appear on the following pages: *Blachan* (page 4); *Coconut Milk* (page 25); *Galangal* (page 8); *Lemon Grass* (page 14); *Sambal* (page 28); and *Tamarind* (page 12).

Weights & Measures

Most of the weights and measures throughout the book are in metric but any ingredient under 25 grams (25 g) or 25 millilitres (25 ml) has been indicated in teaspoons. For those who continue to think and work in Imperial measures there is a quick and simple conversion to keep in mind. That is to take 25 grams as being equal to 1 ounce and 25 millilitres to 1 fluid ounce. However this is not a precise conversion and, while quite satisfactory for small quantities, tends to become less practical as weights and measures increase. The table opposite shows the nearest gram/millilitre equivalent for 1 to 20 ounces/fluid ounces and indicates the difference between the Imperial and U.S. pint. A measuring cup is roughly the equivalent of 225 millilitres.

Ounces/fluid ounces	Approx. g. and ml. to nearest whole figure	Ounces/fluid ounces	Approx. g. and ml. to nearest whole figure
1	28	11	311
2	57	12	340
3	85	13	368
4	113	14	396
5	142	15	428
6	170	16 (American pint)	456
7	198	17	484
8	226	18	512
9	255	19	541
10	283	20 (Imperial pint)	569

SOUPS

Sop Kepiting (crab soup)

1 fresh mangrove crab, about 600 g
1 large onion
2 cloves garlic
20 mm knob fresh ginger
1 fresh red chilli
2 stalks lemon grass
2 carrots
2 sticks celery
1 leek
75 g butter
salt to taste
freshly ground black pepper
1.5 litres fish stock
fresh parsley leaves

serves 6

Cook the crab in rapidly boiling; salted water until it turns a deep pink. Remove, crack claws and cut the body into pieces. Slice the onion, chop the garlic, ginger, chilli and lemon grass and cut the carrots, celery and leeks into julienne strips. Heat the butter in a larger pan and sauté the onion and garlic for 3 minutes, then add the pieces of crab and stir-fry for 5 minutes. Add the ginger, chilli, lemon grass and remaining vegetables and season to taste with salt and freshly ground black pepper. Stir well and cook for a further 3 minutes. Then, heat the stock and, when almost boiling, pour over the crab. Bring to a rapid boil, then lower heat and allow to simmer for a further 4-5 minutes, stirring frequently. To serve: pour into a soup tureen and float the parsley leaves on top.

Soto Babat Jakarta (tripe soup)

400 g tripe
½ teaspoon salt
¼ teaspoon white pepper
2 teaspoons lemon juice
2 tomatoes
2 sticks celery
2 shallots
2 cloves garlic
15 mm knob fresh ginger
15 mm knob galangal
4 fresh red chillies
1 stalk lemon grass
75 ml oil
25 ml dark soya sauce
2 teaspoons brown sugar
2 teaspoons crispy fried onion

serves 4-6

Parboil the tripe, then remove from the water, drain well and cut into small pieces. Place in a shallow dish, season with salt and white pepper and sprinkle the lemon juice on top. Place in the refrigerator and leave for 1 hour. Cut the tomatoes and celery into small dice and slice the shallots. Chop finely the garlic, ginger, galangal, chillies and lemon grass, and pound these together with a small quantity of cold water to form a smooth paste. Heat the oil in a large saucepan, add the shallot and sauté for 4-5 minutes, then add the spice paste, soya sauce and sugar, and continue to cook over a medium heat for 5 minutes, stirring frequently. Pour in the stock and bring to the boil, then add the tripe and adjust seasonings to taste. Lower heat and allow soup to simmer until the tripe is tender, then add the tomato and celery and cook for a further 3 minutes. Transfer to a soup tureen and garnish with crispy fried onion.

Blachan:	A pungent paste made from dried shrimps and spices. Has a very distinctive flavour and there is really no acceptable substitute. Is sold in small slabs and may be stored for lengthy periods in an air-tight container. It is generally obtainable from Asian provision stores.

Sayur Asam (hot and sour vegetable soup)

3 carrots
1 small green pepper
100 g eggplant
1 small cauliflower
75 g string beans
1 onion
2 fresh red chillies
2 macadamia nuts
1 teaspoon blachan (shrimp paste)
1.5 litres beef stock
25 ml tamarind water
2 salem leaves
25 g soft brown sugar
salt to taste
freshly ground white pepper
fresh celery leaves

serves 4-6

Slice the carrots, cut the green pepper and eggplant into small pieces and break the cauliflower into florets. Cut the beans into 30 mm lengths. Chop the onion and chillies and pound these together with the macadamia nuts and blachan to form a smooth paste (use a small amount of cold water if necessary). Pour the stock into a large saucepan and bring to the boil. Add the spice paste, tamarind water, salem leaves and brown sugar and season to taste with salt and freshly ground white pepper. Stir well and allow to simmer over a medium heat for 1 hour. Then, remove and strain into a fresh pan. Add the vegetables and bring back to the boil. Lower heat and simmer until the vegetables are tender but still 'crispy'. To serve: pour into a soup tureen and float the celery leaves on top.

Sop Kimlo Ayam (chicken and shrimp ball soup)

1 small chicken
125 g fresh shrimps
3 dried black mushrooms
2 potatoes
2 shallots
2 small carrots
2 sticks celery
2 cloves garlic
2 eggs
25 g cornstarch
½ teaspoon salt
freshly ground black pepper
oil for deep frying
1 teaspoon nutmeg
25 ml dark soya sauce
2 teaspoons vinegar

serves 4-6

Prepare the chicken and place in a suacepan. Add 1.5 litres of cold water, bring to the boil and cook until the chicken is tender. De-bone the chicken, remove the skin and cut the meat into small cubes. Reserve the cooking stock. Shell and de-vein the shrimps, set half on one side and pound the remainder. Soak the mushrooms in warm water for 30 minutes, then discard the stems and cut the caps into fine shreds. Parboil the potatoes, then cut into thin slices. Slice the shallots, cut the carrot and celery into julienne strips and crush the garlic. Beat the eggs lightly, add the pounded shrimp, garlic, cornstarch, salt and freshly ground black pepper and mix to form a smooth paste (if the paste is too liquid, add a little extra cornstarch), then shape into small balls. Heat the oil in a large pan and deep fry the shrimp balls, then remove, drain off excess oil and set aside. Pour off most of the oil from the pan, then add the shallot and sauté for 4-5 minutes, until golden and crispy. Remove, drain thoroughly and place into a soup tureen, together with the chicken, shrimp balls, fresh shrimps, potato, mushroom, carrot and celery. Bring the reserved stock back to the boil, add nutmeg, soya sauce and vinegar and adjust seasonings to taste. Lower heat and allow stock to simmer for 10 minutes, then pour into the tureen and garnish with chopped celery leaves.

Soto Ayam (spicy chicken soup)

2 chicken breasts
300 g beansprouts
50 g tapioca noodles
20 mm knob fresh ginger
4 cloves garlic
2 teaspoons chopped celery leaves
1 teaspoon turmeric powder
8 black peppercorns
1.5 litres chicken stock
75 ml oil
2 hard boiled eggs
½ lemon

Sambal:
6 fresh red chillies
25 ml vinegar
½ teaspoon sugar
¼ teaspoon salt

Boil the chicken, remove the skin and shred the meat. Lightly boil the beansprouts and tapioca noodles, then drain and set to one side. Chop the ginger and half the garlic and cut the remaining garlic into thin slices. Pound the chopped ginger and garlic together with the turmeric, peppercorns and a little chicken stock to form a smooth paste. Heat the oil and fry the sliced garlic until it becomes golden and crispy, then remove from oil and set to one side. Re-heat the oil and stir-fry the spice paste for 5 minutes, then add the chicken stock and bring back to the boil. Stir well, lower heat and allow to simmer for 30 minutes. Cut the hard boiled eggs into wedges and slice the lemon and place both in a soup tureen, together with the beansprouts, noodles, shredded chicken and celery leaves. Pour the boiling soup into the tureen and serve with side dishes of sambal.

To make the sambal: boil the chillies for a few minutes, until they soften slightly, then pound to a pulp. Add the vinegar, sugar and salt and stir to dissolve.

Sop Buntot (oxtail soup)

800 g oxtail
3 carrots
2 sticks celery
1 leek
2 onions
2 shallots
25 ml vegetable oil
25 g butter
1.5 litres beef stock
salt to taste
freshly ground black pepper

serves 6

Wash and joint the oxtail. Slice 2 carrots, 1 stick of celery and the leek. Chop the onions and remaining carrot and celery. Slice the shallots and fry in the oil until crispy and golden. Heat the butter in a large saucepan, add the chopped vegetables and stir-fry until soft. Then, add the oxtail and stir to brown on all sides. Pour in the stock, season to taste with salt and freshly ground black pepper and bring to the boil. Cover the pan, lower heat and cook slowly for 2 hours. (During the cooking time remove any scum that forms on the surface.) Remove the oxtail and trim off all the meat. Discard the bones. Bring the stock back to the boil, add the sliced vegetables and cook for a further 5-6 minutes, then replace the meat, stir well and pour into individual soup bowls. Garnish with crispy fried shallot.

SEAFOODS

Kepiting Pedas (crab in spicy sauce)

2 large fresh crabs
1 small brown onion
2 shallots
8 fresh red chillies
25 mm knob fresh ginger
15 mm knob fresh galangal
15 mm knob turmeric
2 stalks lemon grass
4 macadamia nuts
salt to taste
freshly ground black pepper
50 ml oil
750 ml thick coconut milk

serves 4

Clean the crabs and partly cook in rapidly boiling water for 6-7 minutes. Then, remove the claws and smash slightly and chop the crab-backs into pieces. Chop, very finely, the onion, shallots, chillies, ginger, galangal, turmeric, lemon grass and macadamia nuts and pound these together with salt, freshly ground black pepper and 2 teaspoons of cold water to form a smooth paste. Heat the oil in a saucepan and stir-fry the spice paste for 5 minutes, then add the coconut milk and bring to the boil. Add the pieces of crab, lower heat and allow to simmer until the crab is well cooked and the sauce is thick. Transfer the crab to a large serving dish and pour the sauce on top. Serve with chunks of bread to dip in the remaining sauce.

Bakwan Udang (shrimp fritters)

200 g fresh baby shrimps
2 shallots
1 leek
1 clove garlic
600 ml vegetable oil
75 g flour
½ teaspoon salt
2 eggs
freshly ground black pepper

serves 4

Shell and de-vein the shrimps. Chop the shallots and leek and crush the garlic. Heat a little oil in a shallow pan and sauté the shrimps until they turn pink. Remove and set aside. Clean the pan, add a little more oil, and sauté the shallot for 3 minutes, then add the leek and garlic and continue to stir-fry for a further 3-4 minutes. Remove and set aside. Sift the flour and salt into a large bowl and make a well in the centre. Break the eggs into the well and beat to produce a smooth, thick batter, using a little water if necessary. Add the shrimps and vegetables to the batter, season with freshly ground black pepper and stir to blend thoroughly. Heat the oil until it starts to smoke, then drop in spoonfuls of the batter and deep fry until golden and crispy. Serve as a main course with rice and vegetables or as a snack.

Galangal:	A member of the ginger family, seldom found outside South East Asia. It is used widely in regional cooking, often in addition to ginger rather than as a substitute. However if galangal is not available use a slightly larger quantity of fresh ginger than is called for in the original.

Cumi-Cumi Panir (deep fried squid)

600 g fresh squid
25 ml fresh lime juice
2 teaspoons sesame oil
25 ml soya sauce
¼ teaspoon salt
¼ teaspoon white pepper
2 eggs
50 g breadcrumbs
oil for deep frying

serves 4

Wash the squid under cold running water and dry thoroughly. Cut the squid down the centre, open out into flat pieces and make criss-cross incisions in the flesh. Sprinkle on the lime juice, sesame oil and soya sauce and season with salt and white pepper. Set aside for 30 minutes. Beat the eggs lightly and pour over the squid. Allow to stand for a further 5 minutes, then coat the squid with breadcrumbs. Heat the oil until it begins to smoke, then deep fry the squid until tender. Serve with rice and green vegetables.

Cumi-Cumi Isi (stuffed squid)

500 g fresh squid
350 g snapper fillets
1 clove garlic
2 egg whites
½ teaspoon salt
¼ teaspoon white pepper
dash of nutmeg
2 shallots
2 fresh red chillies
3 candlenuts
2 stalks lemon grass
oil for frying
250 ml thin coconut milk

serves 4

Wash the squid under cold running water and dry thoroughly. Remove the skin from the snapper (ensure no bones remain) and cut the meat into tiny pieces. Crush the garlic. Beat the egg whites lightly, add the snapper and garlic and season with salt, white pepper and nutmeg. Stir to blend thoroughly, then stuff the mixture into the squid. Chop the shallots, chillies, candlenuts and lemon grass, then sauté in very hot oil for 3-4 minutes. Add the coconut milk and bring to the boil, then lower heat and add the stuffed squid. Allow to simmer until the squid is very tender, then transfer to a serving dish and pour the sauce on top.

Cumi-Cumi Bakar (barbecued squid)

800 g fresh squid
4 shallots
2 small green chillies
2 cloves garlic
25 ml peanut oil
25 ml rice wine
50 ml sweet soya sauce
2 teaspoons soft brown sugar
salt to taste
freshly ground white pepper

serves 4-6

Wash the squid under cold running water and dry throughly. Cook over very hot charcoal, then cut into bite-size pieces and place in a serving dish. Keep warm. Finely chop the shallots, chillies and garlic. Heat the oil and sauté half the shallot until it is soft, then remove, drain and add to the squid. Place the remaining shallot in a small saucepan, add the chilli, garlic, wine, soya sauce and sugar, stir well and bring to the boil. Season to taste with salt and freshly ground white pepper, lower heat and allow to simmer for 3-4 minutes, stirring frequently. Pour the sauce over the squid and serve immediately.

Sambal Goreng Udang (sautéed prawns in coconut milk)

750 g large prawns
2 ripe tomatoes
1 onion
4 shallots
2 cloves garlic
15 mm knob fresh ginger
8 fresh red chillies
4 macadamia nuts
50 ml oil
1 teaspoon turmeric powder
500 ml thick coconut milk
salt to taste
freshly ground black pepper
1 teaspoon chopped coriander leaves

Shell and de-vein the prawns, leaving the tails intact. Skin the tomatoes and chop the flesh into small dice. Chop the onion and shallots, crush the garlic, finely slice the ginger and chillies and grind the macadamia nuts. Heat the oil and sauté the onion and shallot until they become translucent, then remove and pound together with the garlic, ginger, chillies, macadamia nuts and turmeric powder. If necessary, use a little cold water to form a smooth paste. Re-heat the oil and stir-fry the spice-powder for 4-5 minutes, until it begins to give off a fragrant aroma, then add the prawns and stir-fry for 2-3 minutes so that the prawns are thoroughly coated with the spices. Next, add the coconut milk, season to taste with salt and freshly ground black pepper and bring to the boil. Lower heat and allow to simmer until the prawns are cooked and the sauce has reduced considerably. Transfer to a serving dish and garnish with chopped coriander leaves.

Karee Udang (prawn curry)

1 kilo medium size prawns
4 red chillies
2 shallots
1 clove garlic
20 mm knob fresh ginger
15 mm knob fresh langkuas
4 candlenuts
1 teaspoon coriander powder
1 teaspoon cumin powder
1 teaspoon turmeric powder
½ teaspoon salt
100 ml vegetable oil
600 ml thick coconut milk
1 teaspoon chopped celery leaves

serves 4-6

Shell and de-vein the prawns, leaving the tails intact. Boil the chillies for a few minutes, then chop finely. Chop the shallots, garlic, ginger and langkuas and grind these together with the chilli, candlenuts, spice powders and salt. Add a little of the oil to form a smooth paste. Heat the remaining oil in a pan and stir-fry the spice paste for 5-6 minutes, then add the prawns and pour in 250 ml of water. Bring to the boil and cook, over a fairly high heat, for 15 minutes, then add the coconut milk and bring back to the boil. Lower heat and allow to simmer for a further 15-20 minutes, until the sauce thickens. Transfer to a serving dish and sprinkle the chopped celery leaves on top.

Ikan Pepes (fish wrapped in banana leaves)

4 fish fillets, about 125 g each
2 shallots
2 cloves garlic
1 fresh red chilli
15 mm knob fresh ginger
1 candlenut
2 teaspoons turmeric powder
25 g palm sugar
25 g blachan (shrimp paste)
25 ml tamarind water
salt to taste
freshly ground black pepper
4 squares banana leaf

serves 4

Remove all skin from the fish and make sure no bones remain. Finely chop the shallots, garlic, chilli and ginger and grate the candlenut. Heat the oil in a pan and sauté the shallot and garlic for 2 minutes, then add the chilli and ginger and continue to cook for a further 3 minutes, stirring frequently. Add the grated candlenut, turmeric powder, sugar, blachan and tamarind water and season to taste with salt and freshly ground black pepper. Stir to blend well and cook for 3 more minutes, then remove from heat. Place a piece of fish in the centre of each square of banana leaf and spoon a little of the spice mixture on top. Fold the leaves like envelopes and secure with toothpicks. Place the wrapped fish in a steamer and cook for 5 minutes, then transfer to a hot grill (or charcoal barbecue) and cook on each side for 10 minutes. Serve immediately with the folds facing upwards.

Ikan Asap Santan (smoked fish with coconut milk)

800 g smoked fish fillets
4 shallots
2 large tomatoes
2 cloves garlic
25 mm knob fresh ginger
2 stalks lemon grass
2 fresh red chillies
1 candlenut
¼ teaspoon turmeric powder
50 ml oil
salt to taste
freshly ground black pepper
750 ml thin coconut milk
200 ml thick coconut milk
1 teaspoon chopped basil leaves

serves 4

Cut the fish into bite-size chunks. Slice the shallots and tomatoes. Finely chop the garlic, ginger, lemon grass, chillies and candlenut, and pound these together with the turmeric powder and a small quantity of cold water to form a smooth paste. Heat the oil in a large pan and stir-fry the spice paste for 3-4 minutes, then add the shallot and continue to cook over a medium heat until the shallot becomes soft. Then add the fish and tomato, pour in the thin coconut milk, season to taste with salt and freshly ground black pepper and bring to the boil. Allow to boil rapidly for 3 minutes, then lower heat and cook slowly for 35-40 minutes. Finally, add the thick coconut milk, stir well and continue to cook for a further 10 minutes. Transfer to a serving dish, sprinkle the chopped basil leaves on top and serve with plain rice.

Tamarind:	An acid-tasting fruit used to add a sour taste to numerous dishes. Sometimes the fruit itself is used and pounded together with other spices. Alternatively the fruit is soaked in warm water for approximately 15 minutes and the liquid strained through a fine sieve. This is known as tamarind water.

Ikan Bumbu Taocho (spicy fried fish fillets)

600 g fish fillets
1 teaspoon salt
25 ml fresh lemon juice
2 shallots
1 leek
1 clove garlic
2 fresh red chillies
1 fresh green chilli
25 mm knob fresh ginger
50 g flour
oil for deep frying
300 ml thick coconut milk
50 ml taocho (bean sauce)
25 ml tamarind water
50 g palm sugar (soft brown sugar)

serves 4

Remove all skin from the fish and make sure no bones remain. Place the fillets in a shallow dish, season with salt and lemon juice and set aside for 10 minutes. Chop the shallots and leek, crush the garlic and cut the chillies and ginger into julienne strips. Remove the fish from the marinade, pat dry and coat with flour. Heat the oil until it starts to smoke, then deep fry the fish fillets until the outsides are golden and crispy. Remove and drain. Pour a little of the oil into a fresh pan and sauté the shallot and garlic for 3-4 minutes, then add the coconut milk and bring to the boil. Add the leek, chilli, ginger, taocho, tamarind water and palm sugar and stir well. Bring back to the boil, add the pieces of fish and cook for a further minute, then serve immediately.

Ikan Santan (tuna in coconut milk)

800 g tuna fish fillets
2 onions
2 tomatoes
2 leeks
2 fresh red chillies
2 stalks lemon grass
20 mm knob lemon root (optional)
50 ml vegetable oil
3 curry leaves
25 ml fresh lemon juice
700 ml thick coconut milk
salt to taste
freshly ground black pepper

serves 4

Remove any skin from the fish, make sure no bones remain, and cut the flesh into bite-size chunks. Coarsely chop the onions, tomatoes and leeks and finely chop the chillies, lemon grass and lemon root. Heat the oil in a large pan and sauté the onion for 4 minutes, then add the chilli, lemon grass, lemon root, curry leaves, lemon juice and coconut milk. Stir well and bring to the boil, then add the fish, tomato and leek and season to taste with salt and freshly ground black pepper. Lower heat and allow to simmer, stirring occasionally, until the fish is cooked. Serve with steamed rice.

Ikan Asam Padeh (fish in sour sauce)

650 g fish fillets
2 shallots
25 mm knob fresh ginger
2 cloves garlic
2 fresh red chillies
½ teaspoon turmeric powder
½ teaspoon tamarind
25 ml dark soya sauce
25 ml vegetable oil
salt to taste
freshly ground black pepper

serves 4

Remove all skin from the fish fillets, ensure that no bones remain and cut into serving-size pieces. Chop, very finely, the shallots, ginger, garlic and chillies and pound these together with the turmeric powder, tamarind and soya sauce. Heat the oil in a shallow pan and stir-fry the spice paste for 4-5 minutes, then add the fish, cover with approximately 200 ml of cold water and bring to the boil. Lower heat, season to taste with salt and freshly ground black pepper and cook over a very low heat. Serve with fresh vegetables and rice.

Ikan Bakar Colo-Colo (barbecued tuna fish)

2 small tuna, about 600 g each
50 ml fresh lemon juice
25 ml sesame oil
1 teaspoon salt
½ teaspoon white pepper

Sauce:
4 shallots
2 cloves garlic
2 fresh red chillies
2 fresh limes
50 ml peanut oil
150 ml dark soya sauce
2 teaspoons sugar

serves 4

Clean the fish, make incisions in the skin and place in a shallow dish. Sprinkle the lemon juice and sesame oil over the fish and season with salt and white pepper. Set aside in a refrigerator for 1 hour, then cook over hot charcoal and serve with prepared sauce.

To make the sauce: cut the shallots into thin slices, crush the garlic and chop the chillies finely. Peel the limes, remove seeds and chop up the flesh. Heat the oil in a small pan and fry half the sliced shallot until it is golden and crispy. Then, remove and drain off excess oil. Place all the remaining ingredients in a bowl and blend thoroughly. Transfer to individual dishes, top with the fried shallot and serve as a dip.

Ikan Acar Kuning (tuna with pickle sauce)

2 small tuna, about 600 g each
50 ml lemon juice
1 teaspoon salt
½ teaspoon white pepper
oil for deep frying

Sauce:
4 shallots
25 mm knob fresh ginger
2 cloves garlic
2 stalks lemon grass
2 curry leaves
2 candlenuts
¼ teaspoon turmeric powder
2 fresh red chillies
1 carrot
30 mm piece cucumber
50 ml vegetable oil
25 g sugar
salt to taste
50 ml vinegar
400 ml thick coconut milk

serves 4

Clean the fish, make incisions in the skin and place in a shallow dish. Sprinkle the lemon juice over the fish, season with salt and white pepper and set aside in the refrigerator for 1 hour. Heat the oil until it begins to smoke and deep-fry the fish. Drain off excess oil, arrange the fish on a serving dish and pour the prepared sauce on top.

To make the sauce: chop the shallots and ginger and crush the garlic. Chop the lemon grass, curry leaves and candlenuts and place in a mortar. Add the turmeric powder and 25 ml of cold water and pound to produce a thick paste. Cut the chillies, carrot and cucumber into julienne strips. Heat the oil in a pan and sauté the shallot, ginger and garlic for 3 minutes, then add the spice paste and continue to cook for a further 3 minutes, stirring continuously. Add the sugar and salt and pour in the vinegar and coconut milk. Stir to blend thoroughly and bring to the boil. Lower heat and simmer for 10 minutes, then add the vegetables julienne and continue to simmer for a final 5 minutes before pouring over the fish.

Lemon grass: An aromatic grass with a small bulbous root which when crushed gives a strong lemon flavour. Its Indonesian name is sereh and it is readily available in most major spice shops in powdered form as sereh or seria.

POULTRY

Bebek Betutu (steamed stuffed duckling)

2 young ducklings
1 teaspoon salt
1 teaspoon black pepper
2 shallots
25 mm knob fresh ginger
2 fresh red chillies
1 stalk lemon grass
2 lemon leaves
2 cloves garlic
3 candlenuts
75 ml vegetable oil
1 teaspoon blachan (shrimp paste)
2 teaspoons turmeric powder
2 teaspoons cardamom powder
1 teaspoon coriander powder
25 g palm sugar
1 bay leaf
banana leaves

serves 4

Prepare the ducklings and season, inside and out, with salt and black pepper. Slice the shallots, finely chop the ginger, chillies, lemon grass and lemon leaves, crush the garlic and grind the candlenuts. Heat the oil in a large pan, add the shallot, ginger and garlic and sauté for 3-4 minutes, then add the chilli, lemon grass, lemon leaf, candlenut, blachan, spice powders, sugar and bay leaf. Stir-fry for 5 minutes, then remove the mixture from the pan and stuff inside the ducklings. Wrap the ducklings securely in banana leaves, place in a steamer and cook until very tender. Finally, remove the banana leaves and place the ducklings in a very hot oven, or under a hot grill, until the skins are golden brown and crispy.

Ayam Bakakak Bumbu Bali (Balinese style barbecued chicken)

4 small chickens, about 1 kilo each
25 ml tamarind oil
salt
freshly ground black pepper
2 shallots
2 spring onions
2 cloves garlic
2 tomatoes
3 fresh red chillies
25 mm knob fresh ginger
1 stalk lemon grass
2 salem leaves
½ teaspoon tamarind
½ teaspoon blachan (shrimp paste)
¼ teaspoon coriander powder
2 teaspoons sugar
25 ml dark soya sauce
75 ml oil
750 ml chicken stock

serves 4

Clean and prepare the chickens, cut along the underside and flatten with a kitchen hammer. Place skewers through each chicken to keep flat while cooking. Brush both sides of the chicken with tamarind oil and season with salt and freshly ground black pepper. Set aside for 30 minutes. Chop the shallots, spring onions and garlic and cut the tomatoes into small dice. Chop the chillies, ginger, lemon grass, salem leaves, tamarind and blachan and pound these together with the coriander powder, sugar and soya sauce to produce a smooth paste. Heat the oil and sauté the shallot, spring onion and garlic for 4-5 minutes, then add the spice paste and cook for a further 5 minutes, stirring frequently. Next, pour in the stock, add the diced tomatoes, adjust seasonings to taste and bring to the boil. Lower heat and allow to simmer for 15 minutes, then use to brush over both sides of the chickens. Cook the chickens over red-hot charcoal until tender, basting occasionally with the sauce. To serve; transfer the chickens to individual plates and pour the remaining sauce into bowls, to be used as a dip.

Ayam Paniki (barbecued spiced chicken)

1 chicken, about 1.5 kilos
2 shallots
2 fresh red chillies
15 mm knob fresh ginger
½ teaspoon turmeric powder
½ teaspoon salt
freshly ground black pepper
2 stalks lemon grass
25 ml vegetable oil
1 bay leaf
125 ml thick coconut milk

serves 4-6

Prepare the chicken and cut into serving-size pieces. Finely chop the shallots, chillies and ginger and pound together with the turmeric, salt, pepper and a little water to form a smooth paste. Cut the lemon grass into short lengths. Heat the oil in a large pan, add the spice paste and stir-fry for 3 minutes, then add the lemon grass, bay leaf and coconut milk and adjust seasonings to taste. Bring to the boil, add the pieces of chicken and allow to simmer slowly until the chicken is half cooked. Transfer the chicken to a barbecue and finish cooking over hot charcoal.

Ayam Setan (spicy chicken)

2 small chickens
2 onions
3 shallots
15 mm knob fresh ginger
2 fresh red chillies
1 small green chilli
1 clove garlic
oil for deep frying
50 ml sweet soya sauce
25 ml fresh lemon juice
150 ml chicken stock
2 curry leaves
2 teaspoons blachan (shrimp paste)
salt to taste
freshly ground black pepper
25 g chopped spring onion

serves 4

Prepare the chickens and cut into quarters. Chop the onions, shallots and ginger, cut the chillies into very thin slices and crush the garlic. Heat the oil and deep fry the chicken until it is three-quarters cooked, then remove and set aside. Pour a little of the oil into a large frying pan, or wok, add the onion, shallot, ginger, chilli and garlic and stir-fry for 5 minutes, then add the soya sauce, lemon juice, stock, curry leaves and blachan and bring to the boil. Stir well, season to taste with salt and freshly ground black pepper and add the pieces of chicken. Continue to cook over a medium heat until the chicken is very tender, then transfer to a serving dish and garnish with chopped spring onions.

Perkedel Ayam (chicken patties)

½ kilo cooked chicken
200 g potatoes
2 shallots
1 leek
2 sticks celery
2 cloves garlic
1 egg
oil for frying
½ teaspoon salt
freshly ground black pepper

serves 4

De-bone the chicken, remove all skin and pass the meat through a mincer. Boil the potatoes, mash and allow to cool. Chop the shallots, leek and celery very finely and crush the garlic. Beat the egg with a little water. Heat a small quantity of oil and sauté the shallot and garlic for 2 minutes, then add the leek and celery and continue to stir-fry for a further 3 minutes. Remove the vegetables from the pan, allow to cool slightly and place in a mixing bowl. Add the chicken and potato and season with salt and freshly ground black pepper. Then, blend thoroughly, shape into small patties and brush with the egg-wash. Heat the remaining oil, until very hot, then deep fry the patties until they are golden brown. Serve immediately with a green salad.

Sambal Goreng Hati Ayam (chicken livers in hot sauce)

800 g chicken livers
400 g small new potatoes
1 onion
2 shallots
20 mm knob fresh ginger
1 clove garlic
75 g butter
2 teaspoons blachan (shrimp paste)
2 teaspoons chilli oil
½ teaspoon coriander powder
1 bay leaf
25 g soft brown sugar
salt to taste
freshly ground black pepper
450 ml thick coconut milk

serves 4-6

Wash the chicken livers and scrape the new potatoes. Chop the onion, shallots and ginger and crush the garlic. Parboil the potatoes and cut into slices. Heat half the butter in a pan and sauté the chicken livers for 2-3 minutes, then add the sliced potato and continue to cook for a further few minutes, until the potatoes are well browned. Remove the livers and potatoes from the pan and set to one side. Add the remaining butter to the pan and sauté the onion, shallot, ginger and garlic until soft and golden. Add the blachan, chilli oil, coriander, bay leaf, sugar, salt and freshly ground black pepper. Stir-fry for 3-4 minutes, then replace the livers and potato, pour in the coconut milk and bring to the boil. Stir to blend thoroughly, lower heat and simmer until the liquid has reduced by two-thirds. Remove bay leaf and transfer to a serving dish.

Ayam Bumbu Rujak (spiced chicken in coconut milk)

1 fresh chicken, about 2 kilos
12 red chillies
8 shallots
4 cloves garlic
1 teaspoon blachan (shrimp paste)
½ teaspoon turmeric powder
1 teaspoon sugar
salt to taste
100 ml vegetable oil
300 ml thick coconut milk

serves 4

Prepare the chicken and cut into eight pieces. Boil the chillies for a few minutes until they soften. Slice the chillies, shallots and garlic and grind, together with the blachan, turmeric, sugar, salt and a small quantity of the oil. Heat the remaining oil in a large pan and stir-fry the spice paste for 10 minutes, then add the chicken and the coconut milk, together with a similar quantity of hot water. Bring to the boil and stir well, then lower heat and cook for 40-45 minutes, stirring frequently, until the sauce has thickened and reduced considerably.

MEATS

Babi Asam Manis (sweet and sour fillets of pork)

600 g pork fillet
salt
freshly ground black pepper
50 g cornstarch
4 eggs
2 onions
1 green pepper
4 fresh pineapple rings
2 fresh red chillies
400 ml chicken stock
100 g sugar
50 ml vinegar
½ teaspoon red food colouring
oil for deep frying
fresh coriander leaves

serves 4

Cut the pork into thin slices, season with salt and freshly ground black pepper and dust with half the cornstarch. Beat the eggs lightly and pour over the pork, then set aside in the refrigerator for 1 hour. Chop the onions and green pepper, dice the pineapple and finely chop the chillies. Pour the stock into a saucepan, add the sugar, vinegar, red food colouring and remaining cornstarch and bring to the boil. Lower heat, stir well and allow to simmer until the sugar has completely dissolved and the sauce starts to thicken. Meanwhile, heat the oil until it is very hot and deep-fry the pork slices until cooked and golden brown. Remove the pork and allow to drain. Pour off most of the oil, leaving about 50 ml in the pan. Re-heat this oil and sauté the onion for 3-4 minutes, then add the green pepper, pineapple and chillies and stir-fry, over a moderate heat, for a further 4-5 minutes. Then, adjust seasonings to taste, add the pork and the sauce and bring back to the boil. Cook for a further minute, then transfer to a serving dish and garnish with fresh coriander leaves.

Babi Goreng Asam (stir-fried spare ribs)

1 kilo pork spare ribs
2 onions
25 mm knob fresh ginger
2 fresh red chillies
3 cloves garlic
50 ml oyster sauce
25 ml dark soya sauce
75 ml light soya sauce
2 teaspoons vinegar
2 teaspoons cornstarch
75 ml vegetable oil
100 ml tamarind water
salt to taste
freshly ground black pepper
25 g palm sugar

serves 4-6

Cut the ribs into short lengths of approximately 6 cms. Chop the onions, ginger, chillies and garlic and place in a mortar. Add the oyster sauce, soya sauce, vinegar and cornstarch and pound to a smooth paste. Heat the oil in a large frying pan, add the pork ribs and stir-fry until they are part cooked and well browned on all sides. Then, add the spice paste and stir-fry for a further 2-3 minutes. Pour in the tamarind water together with 50 ml of hot water and season to taste with salt and freshly ground black pepper. Bring to the boil, then lower heat, cover the pan and allow to simmer for 30 minutes. Finally, remove the lid, add the palm sugar and cook over a fairly high heat, stirring continuously, until the sauce has reduced by half. Serve immediately with steamed rice.

Rendang Ginjal (curried kidneys)

450 g ox kidneys
salt
freshly ground black pepper
2 shallots
20 mm knob fresh ginger
4 fresh red chillies
2 cloves garlic
2 large tomatoes
50 ml oil
25 g curry powder
1 litre thick coconut milk

serves 4

Wash the brains, remove the veins, slice and season with salt and white pepper. Finely chop the shallots, chillies, ginger, garlic and candlenuts. Hear the peanut oil in a pan and sauté all the chopped vegetables for 3-4 minutes, then add the chilli oil, saffron and bay leaf and pour in the coconut milk. Bring to the boil and reduce by half, then add the brains. Pour in just sufficient stock to cover the brains and bring back to the boil. Immediately lower heat and simmer gently until the brains are tender. (Take care not to over cook or the brains will break apart.) To serve: remove the bay leaf and transfer to a large dish.

Otak Bumbu Padang (braised veal brains)

750 g veal brains
1 teaspoon salt
½ teaspoon white pepper
3 shallots
2 fresh red chillies
30 mm knob fresh ginger
1 clove garlic
2 candlenuts
50 ml peanut oil
½ teaspoon chilli oil
¼ teaspoon saffron powder
1 bay leaf
100 ml thick coconut milk
chicken stock

serves 4

Wash the brains, remove the veins, slice and season with salt and white pepper. Finely chop the shallots, chillies, ginger, garlic and candlenuts. Heat the peanut oil in a pan and sauté all the chopped vegetables for 3-4 minutes, then add the chilli oil, saffron and bay leaf and pour in the coconut milk. Bring to the boil and reduce by half, then add the brains. Pour in just sufficient stock to cover the brains and bring back to the boil. Immediately lower heat and simmer gently until the brains are tender. (Take care not to over cook or the brains will break apart.) To serve; remove the bay leaf and transfer to a large dish.

Kalio Hati Sapi (calf's liver in spicy sauce)

600 g calf's liver
1 large onion
2 tomatoes
2 cloves garlic
20 mm knob fresh ginger
2 stalks lemon grass
50 ml vegetable oil
25 g curry paste
200 ml thick coconut milk
2 curry leaves
1 teaspoon curry powder
¼ teaspoon coriander powder
¼ teaspoon cumin powder
salt to taste
freshly ground black pepper

serves 4

Cut the liver into slices of medium thickness. Chop the onion, tomatoes, garlic, ginger and lemon grass. Heat the oil in a large pan, add the vegetables and the curry paste and stir-fry for 4-5 minutes, then pour in the coconut milk and bring to the boil. Add the curry leaves, spice powders, salt and freshly ground black pepper. Lower heat and cook for a few minutes, until the mixture starts to thicken. Finally, add the liver and continue to cook over a low heat until the meat is tender. Serve immediately.

Danging Rendang (spicy beef chunks)

600 g lean beef
4 shallots
7 red chillies
15 mm knob fresh ginger
15 mm knob fresh langkuas
4 cloves garlic
300 ml thin coconut milk
50 ml vegetable oil
1 teaspoon coriander powder
½ teaspoon cumin powder
salt to taste
freshly ground black pepper
300 ml thick coconut milk

serves 4

Chop the meat into chunks and place in a bowl. Chop the shallots and place half to one side. Chop the chillies, ginger, langkuas and garlic and grind these together with half the shallot and 50 ml of thin coconut milk. Pour this paste over the meat and stir to ensure an even coating. Set aside for 30 minutes. Then, heat the oil in a large frying pan and sauté the remaining shallot until it softens. Add the meat and the marinade and season with coriander, cumin, salt and freshly ground black pepper. Pour in the remaining thin coconut milk and bring to the boil, stirring continuously, then lower heat and allow to simmer until the meat is tender. Finally, add the thick coconut milk and continue to cook, over a medium heat, until the liquid has been almost completely reduced.

Daging Bumbu Bali (Balinese style sautéed beef)

600 g beef topside
2 shallots
20 mm knob fresh ginger
2 fresh red chillies
2 cloves garlic
3 candlenuts
25 ml oil
2 teaspoons ground ginger
2 teaspoons turmeric powder
1 teaspoon cardamom powder
1 teaspoon coriander powder
½ teaspoon black peppercorns
½ teaspoon blachan (shrimp paste)
2 bay leaves
150 ml thick coconut milk
salt to taste

serves 4-6

Cut the beef into small thin slices. Finely chop the shallots, ginger, chillies and garlic and grate the candlenuts. Heat the oil, add the beef and sauté until well browned. Remove the beef and set to one side. Re-heat the oil and sauté the chopped vegetables for 3-4 minutes, then add the grated candlenut, spice powders, peppercorns, blachan and bay leaves. Stir-fry for a further 3 minutes, then replace the beef and pour in the coconut milk. Add salt to taste and bring to the boil. Lower heat and allow to simmer until the meat is cooked and the sauce has reduced by half. Remove bay leaves and serve with steamed rice and green vegetables.

Daging Tum (chopped beef in banana leaves)

650 g beef topside
25 mm knob fresh ginger
2 fresh red chillies
2 cloves garlic
2 candlenuts
50 ml oil
2 teaspoons ground ginger
2 teaspoons turmeric powder
1 teaspoon coriander powder
½ teaspoon ground cloves
½ teaspoon black peppercorns
salt to taste
banana leaves

serves 4

Finely chop the beef. Shred the ginger, slice the chillies, crush the garlic and grate the candlenuts. Heat the oil in a frying pan, add the ginger, chillies and garlic and sauté for 3-4 minutes, then add the grated candlenut, spice powders, peppercorns and salt to taste. Add the beef, mix well and stir-fry for a further 2-3 minutes, until the meat is completely sealed. Remove mixture from the pan, allow to cool slightly, then divide into four and place portions on banana leaves. Fold like envelopes and secure with toothpicks. Place in a steamer and cook until the beef is tender.

Lapis Daging (fried beef fillets)

450 g rump steak
1 brown onion
2 shallots
20 mm knob galangal
2 cloves garlic
25 g brown sugar
salt
freshly ground black pepper
75 ml dark soya sauce
2 tomatoes
oil for frying

serves 4

Cut the meat into thin slices and flatten even more with a kitchen mallet. Place the meat into a shallow dish. Chop the onion, shallots, galangal and garlic and pound these together with the brown sugar, salt, freshly ground black pepper and a small quantity of cold water to form a smooth paste. Add the soya sauce and blend thoroughly, then pour the mixture over the meat and place in the refrigerator for 2-3 hours. Cut the tomatoes into small dice. Heat the oil in a shallow frying pan and fry the meat until it is browned on both sides. Add the marinade and the tomatoes and continue to cook over a medium heat until the meat is cooked and the sauce is thick. Serve immediately.

Rempah-Rempah (beef and coconut rissoles)

500 g prime beef
300 g grated coconut
20 mm knob fresh ginger
2 cloves garlic
1 teaspoon blachan (shrimp paste)
½ teaspoon coriander powder
½ teaspoon cumin powder
1 teaspoon salt
½ teaspoon white pepper
4 eggs
oil for deep frying

serves 4

Pass the beef through a fine mincer into a mixing bowl. Mix three-quarters of the coconut with a small quantity of warm water until it is well moistened, then add to the beef. Shred the ginger and crush the garlic. Mix the blachan with about 50 ml of water and pound together with the coriander and cumin. Add the spice paste, ginger and garlic to the beef and season to taste with salt and white pepper. Beat the eggs lightly and add to the beef. Knead well until the mixture is smooth and thoroughly blended, then form into small balls, or rissoles, and coat with the remaining grated coconut. Heat the oil until it is very hot and deep fry the beef balls until the outsides are golden and crispy. Drain off excess oil before serving.

Martabak (mutton rolls)

500 g mutton
¼ teaspoon salt
freshly ground white pepper
1 onion
2 shallots
1 stick celery
1 clove garlic
2 teaspoons curry powder
2 eggs
12 spring roll wrappers (or savoury pancakes)
oil for frying

serves 4

Pass the mutton through a fine mincer into a mixing bowl and season with salt and freshly ground white pepper. Chop the onion, shallots and celery very finely and crush the garlic. Add these to the meat together with the curry powder. Beat the eggs lightly and add 2/3 to meat mixture. Stir well. Divide the mixture into twelve equal portions and place in the centre of the wrappers. Roll up and seal with the remaining egg. Heat the oil in a shallow frying pan and fry the rolls, turning occasionally, until they are cooked and golden brown in colour.

Gulai Kambing (spiced lamb)

850 g fresh lamb
2 onions
3 fresh red chillies
20 mm knob fresh ginger
15 mm knob lemon root
1 stalk lemon grass
2 cloves garlic
8 macadamia nuts
2 ripe tomatoes
75 ml vegetable oil
½ teaspoon ground cardamom
½ teaspoon cumin powder
½ teaspoon turmeric powder
¼ teaspoon fennel powder
1 cinnamon stick
4 cloves
salt to taste
freshly ground black pepper
1 litre thick coconut milk

serves 4-6

Cut the lamb into bite-size cubes. Chop the onions, chillies, ginger, lemon root and lemon grass, crush the garlic and grind the macadamia nuts. Skin the tomatoes and cut the flesh into small dice. Heat the oil in a large pan, add the onion, chillies and garlic and sauté until the onion becomes translucent. Then, add the ginger, lemon root, lemon grass and tomato and cook for a further 3 minutes, stirring frequently. Add the spice powders, cinnamon stick and cloves and season to taste with salt and freshly ground black pepper. Pour in the coconut milk and bring to the boil, stirring continuously, then lower heat and allow to simmer until the meat is very tender. Serve immediately with steamed rice.

Coconut milk: This is not the liquid found inside young coconuts which is correctly referred to as coconut water. Coconut milk is obtained by grating the flesh of a mature coconut and squeezing this with water. On average the flesh of one coconut squeezed with 75 ml of water will produce the thick milk referred to most frequently in this edition. To make a thinner milk the process should be repeated one or more times. Where fresh coconuts are not available, the milk may be bought in cans or as a frozen product.

SATE

Indonesian Sate

400 g lean chicken, beef or mutton
4 shallots
15 mm fresh ginger
2 cloves garlic
2 stalks lemon grass
1 teaspoon curry powder
½ teaspoon cumin powder
salt to taste
2 teaspoons brown sugar
25 ml vegetable oil
100 ml thick coconut milk
cucumber wedges
onion wedges

Sate sauce:
8 dried red chillies
2 shallots
2 cloves garlic
4 candlenuts
50 ml peanut oil
50 ml tamarind water
25 g brown sugar
salt to taste
200 g roasted peanuts

Cut the meat into small cubes and thread onto bamboo skewers (about six pieces to each skewer). Chop the shallots, ginger, garlic and lemon grass and place in a mortar. Add the curry powder, cumin powder, salt, sugar and oil and, using a pestle, pound to a smooth paste. (Use an electric grinder, if preferred.) Pour the coconut milk into a shallow dish, add the spice paste and stir to blend thoroughly. Place the skewers of meat into the milk and allow to marinate for 40 minutes, turning occasionally, to ensure the meat is completely coated. Cook over hot charcoal, basting with the remaining marinade. Serve with hot sate sauce and side dishes of cucumber and onion.

To make the sauce: first soak the chillies in warm water until they become soft. Chop the chillies, shallots and garlic and pound together with a teaspoon of peanut oil to produce a smooth paste. Heat the remaining peanut oil in a pan and stir-fry the spice paste for 3-4 minutes, then add the tamarind water, sugar, salt and 200 ml of water and bring to the boil. Crush the peanuts and add to the sauce. Stir to blend thoroughly, lower heat and simmer until the sauce thickens.

RICE & NOODLES

Nasi Purih (steamed rice)

200 g long-grain rice
¼ teaspoon salt
1 teaspoon peanut oil

serves 4-6

First, wash the rice under cold running water, then drain thoroughly. Place the rice into a saucepan and add just sufficient cold water to barely cover. Add the salt and bring to the boil, then lower heat and allow to simmer for 4-5 minutes. Drain the rice thoroughly again and place into individual bowls. Sprinkle a little peanut oil on top of the rice and place the bowls in a container with a tightly fitting lid. Place the container over boiling water and steam until the rice is fluffy, approximately 1 hour.

Nasi Lemak (rice cooked in coconut milk)

300 g long-grain rice
2 shallots
1 clove garlic
20 mm knob fresh ginger
300 ml thick coconut milk
salt to taste
freshly ground black pepper
cucumber slices
fresh pineapple chunks

serves 4

Wash the rice and allow to soak for 4 hours, then drain thoroughly. Place in a saucepan, cover with cold water and bring to the boil. Parboil for 15 minutes, then drain thoroughly again and set aside. Chop the shallots, garlic and ginger very finely. Pour the coconut milk into a large saucepan and bring to the boil. Add the chopped shallot, garlic and ginger and season to taste with salt and freshly ground black pepper. Stir well and cook for 1 minute, then add the partially cooked rice and stir to blend thoroughly. Cook over a fairly high heat, stirring frequently to avoid sticking, until most of the liquid has been absorbed. Then lower heat, place a tightly fitting lid on the pan, and continue to cook until the rice is tender and fluffy. Garnish with slices of cucumber and chunks of pineapple.

Note: Traditionally, Nasi Lemak is served at breakfast time, accompanied by fried shrimps, ikan bilis (small salted fish), grilled pieces of chicken and a sambal.

Sambal: Usually served as a side dish and very popular throughout South East Asia. Is made from grinding chillies, blachan (see page 4) and salt, and, in that form, can be stored for lengthy periods. Just prior to using, the required amount should be blended with sugar and fresh lime or lemon juice. Proportions depend on individual tastes. Is sometimes available in Asian provision stores, and is usually marketed as Sambal Badjak.

Nasi Kuning (rice cooked in coconut milk)

300 g long-grain rice
1 shallot
2 fresh red chillies
25 mm knob fresh ginger
10 mm knob lemon root
2 salem leaves (or bay leaves)
500 ml thin coconut milk
½ teaspoon turmeric powder
salt to taste

serves 4

Soak the rice for 2 hours, then wash under cold running water, drain thoroughly and place into a pan. Chop the shallot, chillies, ginger and lemon root. Pour the coconut milk into a saucepan, add the shallot, chilli, ginger, lemon root and salem leaves, and bring to the boil. Lower heat and allow to simmer slowly for 45 minutes, then strain the liquid, through a fine sieve, over the rice. Add turmeric powder and salt to taste and cover the pan with a tightly fitting lid. Place the pan over boiling water and cook until the rice is tender and fluffy.

Nasi Gurih (spicy white rice)

400 g long-grain rice
1 shallot
20 mm knob fresh ginger
1 clove garlic
6 fresh coriander leaves
1 stalk lemon grass
1 bay leaf
½ teaspoon ground nutmeg
¼ teaspoon ground cloves
salt to taste.

serves 4-6

Wash the rice under cold running water and drain well. Finely chop the shallot, ginger, garlic, coriander leaves and lemon grass. Pour the coconut milk into a saucepan, add all the ingredients except the rice, stir well and bring to the boil. Simmer for 2 minutes, then stir in the rice and bring back to the boil. Lower the heat so that the liquid is barely simmering, then place a lid on the pan and cook for 20 minutes. Remove lid, fluff-up the rice with a fork, then replace lid and cook until the liquid has been completely absorbed. Remove bay leaf before serving.

Mee Kuwah (soup noodles)

2 bundles egg noodles
250 g cooked chicken meat
1 brown onion
2 shallots
25 mm knob fresh ginger
1 leek
1 stick celery
150 g white cabbage
2 cloves garlic
50 ml vegetable oil
1.2 litres chicken stock
salt to taste
freshly ground white pepper
2 teaspoons light soya sauce
2 teaspoons vinegar
25 g sugar

serves 4

Cook the noodles in rapidly boiling water, then drain and place into a large serving dish. Remove any skin from the chicken and cut the meat into shreds. Slice the onion and shallots, chop the ginger, leek and celery and shred the cabbage. Heat the oil and sauté the shallot until it is golden and crispy, then remove from the pan and set to one side. Re-heat the oil and sauté the onion and garlic until the onion is translucent, then add the chicken and ginger, pour in the stock and season to taste with salt and freshly ground white pepper. Bring to the boil, add the leek, celery, soya sauce, vinegar and sugar, stir well and cook over a high heat for 2 minutes. Finally, lower heat and simmer for a further 5 minutes, then pour into the dish containing the noodles. Garnish with the crispy fried shallots and serve immediately.

Nasi Goreng (special fried rice)

850 g long-grain rice
125 g fresh shrimps
100 g chicken meat
100 g fresh mutton
3 eggs
2 shallots
2 cloves garlic
4 fresh red chillies
2 teaspoons blachan (shrimp paste)
50 ml peanut oil
50 ml sweet soya sauce
salt to taste
freshly ground white pepper

serves 4-6

Wash the rice and drain thoroughly, then steam until tender and fluffy. Shell and de-vein the shrimps and halve, lengthways. Chop the chicken meat and mutton and beat the eggs lightly. Chop the shallots, garlic, red chillies and blachan and pound together with one third of the peanut oil to produce a smooth paste. Heat the remaining oil in a pan and stir-fry the spice paste for 3-4 minutes, then add the shrimps, chicken and mutton and season with soya sauce, salt and freshly ground white pepper. Cook over a moderate heat for 8 minutes then increase the heat to high, add the beaten egg and cook, stirring continuously, until the egg begins to set. Finally, add the rice, stir to blend thoroughly, then serve immediately.

Bami Goreng (fried noodles)

300 g fresh noodles
75 g shrimps
75 g cooked chicken meat
50 g beansprouts
75 g leafy green vegetable
2 cloves garlic
50 g vegetable oil
2 eggs
25 ml dark soya sauce
25 ml light soya sauce
salt to taste
freshly ground black pepper

serves 4

Place the noodles into a saucepan of rapidly boiling water and partially cook for 3 minutes, then remove from the pan and drain thoroughly. Shell and de-vein the shrimps and shred the chicken meat. Trim and chop the beansprouts and green vegetable. Chop the garlic very finely. Heat the oil in a large pan and sauté the garlic for 2-3 minutes, then add the shrimps and stir-fry for a further 2 minutes. Break the eggs into the pan and stir, then add the chicken meat, noodles, vegetables, soya sauce, salt and freshly ground black pepper. Stir to blend thoroughly and retain over a medium heat until fully cooked. Serve with chilli sauce and hot pickles.

VEGETABLES & SALADS

Tumis Goreng (Balinese style spinach)

500 g spinach
4 shallots
1 small tomato
2 fresh red chillies
1 clove garlic
25 ml vegetable oil
2 curry leaves
1 teaspoon sugar
½ teaspoon salt
freshly ground black pepper
25 ml light soya sauce
2 teaspoons dark soya sauce
150 clear chicken stock

serves 4-6

Wash the spinach under cold running water, shake dry, then wash again. Cut into short lengths (approximately 60 mm) and cook in a steamer until tender. Chop the shallots, tomato, chillies and garlic. Heat the oil in a large pan and sauté the shallot, chilli and garlic for 3-4 minutes, then add tomato, curry leaves, sugar, salt, freshly ground black pepper, soya suace and stock. Bring to the boil and add spinach. Then, lower heat and cook for a few minutes, turning frequently with a slotted spoon, until the spinach starts to wilt. Remove curry leaves before serving.

Tahu Goreng (fried beancurd)

2 squares fresh beancurd
150 g beansprouts
1 large brown onion
1 small cucumber
2 eggs
¼ teaspoon salt
freshly ground white pepper

Peanut sauce:
150 g roasted peanuts
6 cloves garlic
2 fresh red chillies
25 ml oil
100 ml dark soya sauce
25 ml vinegar
25 g soft brown sugar

serves 4

Cut each of the beancurd squares into six pieces. Trim the beansprouts and parboil in rapidly boiling water for 2 minutes. Cut the onion into fine slices and slice the cucumber. Beat the eggs lightly and season with salt and freshly ground white pepper. Dip the beancurd into the egg. Heat the oil until it is very hot, then fry the beancurd, turning once, to ensure it is well-browned. Then arrange the beancurd on a serving plate, cover with beansprouts and pour the sauce on top. Re-heat the oil and fry the onion until golden and crispy, then sprinkle this over the sauce. Garnish with slices of cucumber.

To make the sauce: grind the peanuts, chop the garlic finely and shred the chillies. Heat the oil and fry the garlic until it is crispy and golden, then add the peanuts, chillies, soya sauce, vinegar, sugar and 100 ml of cold water. Bring to the boil and stir to blend thoroughly, then lower heat and allow to simmer for a further 5 minutes, stirring frequently. Allow the sauce to cool slightly before pouring over the beanspourts.

Asinan Jakarta (sour salad)

250 g salted Chinese cabbage
150 g white cabbage
150 g cucumber
150 g beancurd
100 g beansprouts
2 fresh red chillies
50 g brown sugar
25 ml vinegar
25 ml tamarind water
½ teaspoon salt
½ teaspoon white pepper
50 g chopped roasted peanuts
tomato wedges

serves 4

Shred the cabbage, slice the cucumber and beancurd and trim the beansprouts. Remove the seeds from the chillies, chop into small pieces and pound together with the sugar, vinegar and tamarind water. Place the spice paste in a pan and add 1 litre of cold water. Add salt and pepper and bring to the boil. Stir to blend then strain into a large bowl. Allow to cool slightly, then add the vegetables and beancurd and place in a cool place for 8 hours. To serve; arrange vegetables on a large plate, sprinkle the chopped peanut on top and garnish with tomato wedges.

Sambal Goreng Buncis (green bean sambal)

225 g green beans
1 small tomato
1 onion
2 fresh red chillies
1 stalk lemon grass
50 g chicken livers
3 macadamia nuts
50 ml vegetable oil
75 ml thick coconut milk
salt to taste
freshly ground black pepper

serves 4

Top and tail the beans and cut into 60 mm slices. Skin the tomato and cut the flesh into small dice. Slice the onion and chillies, finely chop the lemon grass and liver and grind the macadamia nuts. Heat the oil and sauté the onion and chilli for 4-5 minutes, until the onion is translucent. Add the tomato, lemon grass, liver and macadamia nuts and cook, over a medium heat, for a further 5 minutes, stirring frequently. Then add the beans, pour in the coconut milk and season to taste with salt and freshly ground black pepper. Bring to the boil, then lower heat and cook slowly for a few minutes, until the beans are tender but still crispy.

Telor Orak-Arik (vegetable omelette)

1 leek
½ small white cabbage
1 stick celery
2 shallots
1 fresh red chilli
1 clove garlic
5 eggs
50 ml vegetable oil
salt to taste
freshly ground black pepper

Shred the leek and cabbage. Chop the celery, shallots, chilli and garlic. Beat the eggs lightly. Heat the oil in a frying pan, add the shallot and garlic and sauté until golden brown in colour, then add the leek, cabbage, celery and chilli and season to taste with salt and freshly ground black pepper. Retain over a medium heat and stir frequently until the vegetables are three-quarters cooked. Finally, pour in the egg and cook until the egg sets. Serve with a green salad.

Gado-Gado

(mixed salad with peanut sauce)

½ small cabbage
150 g beansprouts
100 g green beans
2 potatoes
100 g spinach leaves
100 g beancurd
50 ml peanut oil
1 small cucumber
2 hard boiled eggs
25 g crumbled prawn crisps

Sauce:
2 shallots
2 cloves garlic
2 fresh red chillies
125 g roasted peanuts
1 teaspoon blachan (shrimp paste)
25 ml peanut oil
225 ml tamarind water
25 ml dark soya sauce
25 g soft brown sugar
salt to taste
freshly ground black pepper

serves 4-6

Wash and prepare all the vegetables. Separately, steam the cabbage, beansprouts, green beans, potatoes and spinach until barely cooked (they should be tender but still crispy). Cut the beancurd into thin slices and fry in the oil until golden, then remove and drain off excess oil. Peel and slice the cucumber and quarter the hard boiled eggs. Arrange the cucumber and egg around the edge of a dinner plate, place all the vegetables in the centre and add the slices of fried beancurd. Pour the peanut sauce over the salad and sprinkle the crumbled prawn crisps on top.

To make the sauce: chop finely the shallots, garlic and chillies and grind the peanuts. Chop the blachan into tiny pieces. Heat the oil in a pan and sauté the shallot, garlic, chilli and blachan for 4-5 minutes, then pound into a smooth paste. In a fresh saucepan, bring the tamarind water to the boil, add the peanuts and cook, over a moderate heat, for 15 minutes. Then, add the spice past, dark soya sauce, sugar, salt and freshly ground black pepper, stir to blend thoroughly and cook for a further 10-12 minutes, until the sauce is thick. Allow sauce to cool before pouring over salad.

DESSERTS

Kolak Pisang (stewed bananas with coconut milk)

8 bananas (ripe but firm)
250 g soft brown sugar
100 g white sugar
4 pandan leaves*
25 g cornstarch
1 litre thick coconut milk

serves 4-6

Cut the bananas into slices of about 12 mm thickness and place into a fairly shallow saucepan. Cover with water and slowly bring to the boil. Allow to simmer for a few minutes, then remove the bananas and set to one side. Add the brown and white sugar to the pan, together with the pandan leaves, and bring back to the boil. Stir until the sugar has completely dissolved. Mix the cornstarch with the coconut milk, add to the syrup in the pan and once again bring back to the boil. Finally, place the banana slices back in the pan and allow to simmer gently for a further 3-4 minutes. Remove pandan leaves before serving.

*NOTE: If pandan leaves are not available, add a little green food colouring for the final 3-4 minutes of cooking time.

Naga Sari (steamed bananas)

4 small bananas
150 ml thick coconut milk
125 g rice flour
25 g tapioca flour
50 g sugar
¼ teaspoon salt
banana leaves

serves 4

Cut the bananas into halves, lengthways. Pour the coconut milk into a saucepan and bring to the boil. Add the rice flour, tapioca flour, sugar and salt and stir to blend thoroughly. Allow to simmer over a medium heat until the mixture is very thick. Cut the banana leaves into small squares and lay a piece of banana on top of each. Spoon a little of the mixture on top and fold the leaves carefully, so that they do not split. Secure the leaves with toothpicks and place in a steamer. Cook for 20-25 minutes over rapidly boiling water.

Kue Labu (pumpkin tart)

175 g sweet shortcrust pastry dough
300 g pumpkin
1 egg
100 g sugar
¼ teaspoon cinnamon
¼ teaspoon powdered ginger
pinch of all-spice
pinch of salt
50 g cornstarch
50 g seedless raisins
½ teaspoon powdered nutmeg

Roll out the dough and line a 24 cm baking tin. Trim the edges and use the left-over dough to make 'twists'. Prick the dough with a fork and place in the refrigerator for 1 hour. Clean the pumpkin and cut into small pieces. Cook the pumpkin in a steamer until it is soft, then allow to cool and place in a mixing bowl. Beat the egg lightly and add to the pumpkin, together with the sugar, cinnamon, ginger, all-spice, salt and cornstarch. Then, mix to blend thoroughly. Place a layer of raisins along the bottom of the pastry shell, add the pumpkin mixture and sprinkle the nutmeg on top. Decorate with the pastry 'twists' and bake in a moderate oven.

Wajik (rice cake)

300 g glutinous rice
125 ml thick coconut milk
150 g palm sugar
¼ teaspoon salt
banana leaves

Wash the glutinous rice under cold running water, then place in a bowl of fresh water and allow to soak overnight. Before cooking, rinse again, then steam until well cooked. Pour the coconut milk into a saucepan and bring to the boil. Add the sugar and salt and continue to cook, stirring frequently, until the mixture is thick and oily. Then, add the rice and blend thoroughly. Allow to simmer over a medium heat until very thick, then pour into a shallow dish that has been lined with banana leaves. Allow to cool slightly, then place in a refrigerator for at least 2 hours. Cut into small wedges to serve.

Lapis Legis (spiced layer cake)

6 egg whites
250 g sugar
10 egg yolks
350 g butter
250 g all-purpose flour
½ teaspoon vanilla essence
½ teaspoon cinnamon powder
½ teaspoon nutmeg powder
½ teaspoon all-spice powder

Beat the egg whites with one third of the sugar and, in a separate bowl, beat the egg yolks with another third. Soften the butter and cut into small pieces, then mix this with the remaining sugar and beat until light and creamy. Then, place the three mixtures into one large bowl, add the flour and vanilla essence and blend thoroughly. Transfer two-thirds of the mixture to another bowl and to this add cinnamon, nutmeg and all-spice powder and stir to blend well. Pour one third of the spiced mixture into a well-greased cake tin and bake in a moderate oven until firm, then add half the plain mixture and bake until this is also firm. Repeat the process three more times; spiced, plain and ending with spiced. Turn out on to a wire rack and allow to cool before serving.

Kue Kelepon (coconut rice balls)

600 ml thick coconut milk
½ teaspoon vanilla essence
¼ teaspoon salt
2 pandan leaves
350 g glutinous rice powder
100 g soft brown sugar
75 g finely grated coconut

Pour coconut milk into a saucepan, add vanilla essence, salt and pandan leaves and bring to the boil, then lower heat and allow to simmer for 10 minutes. Remove the pandan leaves and pour liquid into a mixing bowl. Then, add the glutinous rice flour and stir with a wooden spoon until the mixture is smooth and firm (if mixture is not firm enough, add a little more rice flour). Turn the mixture out on to a lightly-floured surface and divide into small portions. Flatten into circles, place a little brown sugar in the centre of each and shape into small balls, approximately 25 mm in diameter. Bring a large pan of water to a rapid boil and add the rice balls. After they rise to the surface, leave for 45 seconds, then remove, pat dry and coat with grated coconut. Allow to cool before serving.

Index (English titles):

The editor and publishers wish to thank the following for their very generous and considerable assistance in compiling the material for this book:
Jakarta Mandarin Hotel, Jakarta Hilton Hotel, Bali Hyatt Hotel, Shinta Indonesian Enterprises (Hong Kong), *Wisma Indonesian Club* (Hong Kong). Also, on a personal level, thanks to Mrs. Rahmiati Santoso who was responsible for supervising the preparation of food for many of the pictures used in the book.

Other books published in this series:
Tastes of: 'Hong Kong', 'Singapore', 'Malaysia', 'Philippines', 'Thailand', 'Sri Lanka' and 'Japan'.